MW01152971

CEREMONY

SLOPE EDITIONS

New Hampshire   New York   Massachusetts

CEREMONY

Winner of the 2012 Slope Editions Book Prize

Mary Austin Speaker

ISBN: 978-0-9885221-0-7

First Edition

Library of Congress Cataloging-In-Publication Data

Speaker, Mary Austin, 1977-
  [Poems. Selections]
  CEREMONY / Mary Austin Speaker. -- First edition.
      pages cm
  Poems.
  Winner of the 2012 Slope Editions Book Prize.
  ISBN 978-0-9885221-0-7
  I. Title.
  PS3619.P3728C47 2013
  811'.6--dc23

Designed by Mary Austin Speaker.

This book was set in Old Style 7, designed
by the Miller and Richard Foundry in 1907.

for Chris Martin

CONTENTS

II.

TO INHABIT

III.
YOU CAN HAVE IT ALL

IV.
NUMEROUSNESS

CEREMONY BY MARY AUSTIN SPEAKER

Matthea Harvey

This book arrives in a shimmery white envelope, woven of strongest spider silk, impossible to open. If, however, you whisper, "yes" to it, it opens of its own accord and showers you with snow. A handbook called *The New Rules of Causality* in which "hillsides follow lions" lands at your ankle, a Word Kaleidoscope rolls down the hall. Reach in to dig out the tiny boxes lodged in the far corner of the package. They are labeled "mystery" and "hope."

How to talk about a book that delves into mystery head-on? Maybe by tracking how it bewilders (indeed, there is a poem titled "Bewilderment.") Speaker's short, sometimes unpunctuated lines allow you to track her myriad transformations, things we couldn't see without the poet's magnifying glass: "this too / is exhaling: particles moving off / in their tiny boats, violet and charged // toward each pole..." Her lyrics revel in the personification of the natural world (trees have wrists "whitened with wind") and words ("a flood of yes"), but also the reverse: "Our fingers grew restless // and skittered over tabletops, like mice."

In the section, "You Can Have It All," the language of one poem sprouts into four, "When you have birds in you // they are red" morphs into "When birds are in you they are // two boys playing basketball but it is really you and me who are / positioning themselves in the field" and "When you have birds in you they are // an offering to the sidewalks, or perhaps a performance..." This remixing gives this reader the pleasurable sense that each poem in *Ceremony* exists in infinite variations—a version of the many-worlds theory in poetry.

Speaker's work offers so many delights—tiny tide pools of rhyme, the abstract made concrete, the concrete made uncertain. In "Origin Story" she writes, "Dreaming became us," and the doubled nature of that statement is exactly what this book enacts. We enjoy how dreaming makes us look, but also how it makes us *look*.

I.

THE FIELD OF UNSPEAKABLE COLOR

ORIGIN STORY

It began with a walk in the woods.
The weather became us.

We came to find the owls
who became trees.

Feathers whitened
the corners of our room

which became our winter habits.
So we invented songs

which became the animals
who abided unseen

in a house that reason left
every time we travelled

into ourselves. When we awoke
our arms were crossed

over our chests like bats.
Dreaming became us.

Only the movies delivered us
from a winter of no color.

We turned on the snow.
We turned on no.

Yes became us
like forever and sunsmell

like patterns and lace
not ever about whether

the world was good or bad
because it was only both.

This is why
we followed the animals

and the animals
followed us back.

THE PRIVATE ANIMAL

In the movies
when people turn

into animals
the animal self

pushes through the soft
human body

so the human
becomes a soft side

carried around
inside the animal self

to be appealed to
by other humans

in emergencies
which makes a good story

as we sit in our seats
folded like dogs

or baboons considering
our own private animals

even the not quite
two year old boy

having a shape that sings
a song he knows and lives

as any body does
burrowing with fur

into the self-shaped spaces
it's carved out for itself.

I am still haunted
by a black van passing

its back doors opening
and men inside

with dark glasses
all-black suits

and horrible guns
protecting the president.

I am still haunted because
my own private animal

had just seen
the shape of the President

a slender shadow
against a tinted window

of a limousine
and it was feeling

a little sentimental
my own private animal

surfacing in the sunshine
flooding Park

while the President
drove by

followed by the van
and then its doors

snapping open
and there they were

with their horrible guns
just like in movies

when a crime is just
about to happen

the air charged
with suspense.

What charged air
must the president

move through
while he considers

the shape of his own
private animal

a regal thing with claws
a coat of fur

too thick to admit
intruders.

Some of us
are scale and claw.

Some shed our skin
rear up and snort

or burrow our way
into trees.

Some of us graze drunk
on soporific fruit.

And some of us are fish
or shaped like stars

or armadillos or gulls
hanging in a constant wake.

THE TALKING THAT PLACES MAKE

As awkwardly as
always this city

will grow
after I and everyone

leave it
gets taller

cranes with their
pelican bills

swallowing air
light

placing each iron
twig in a notch

of its nest
til it's ready

to put by
its babies

little dreamers of flight
tucked into desks

quarrels
packets of sugar

if I or everyone
knew how to stop

increasing
we could sing

all at once
our very

separate sounds
but the air around us

won't stop
so we throw

our baseballs and hay
our bombshells trailing

each other like days
following following

I and everyone
in the everyone song

together
we can do anything

THE FIELD OF UNSPEAKABLE COLOR

No one had said
how to thrive

so we lived packed in
incandescent

peopling the romance
of matches and dusk

to resound in a pocket of wind
was to perform our formlessness

unidentified feathers
among the petroglyphs

receipts littering
the stadium's slope

we watched our backs
watching others watch us

and our looking
became a fabric

a flag
we sewed

our doors together
to make it brighter

stronger
we stood

in a field
of unspeakable color

SCALE FOR AN IDEAL CITY

We who know
how to return

and do not do so
place ourselves

between plant-life
and light or glisten

in our beds
and surface

to our thousand
open doors

to again
and again

so we sort
our fortunes

hurl the economy
of starlings aloft

til the sky is so distracted
they stay

high dark clouds
passing overhead

unperturbed
this

is an argument
for the small

emphatic city
welcome stranger

LEAVETAKINGS

When we have left
for elsewhereness

for gold of other
houses' bricks

and steam-flushed
smoke of other stacks

the mint-curled
stems of other

blooms push
centerfolds

to brighten
stranger medians

blurs trick by
teaching us to look

into the places
we can know

as much as we
can know an animal

that is almost
and not at all

our patterns briar
with alleyway and bay

when elsewhere's frank
and ifless light

demarks its residents
with present tense

stepping onto walks
riding red bicycles

even those
who hunker

forth in snow
toward something

surer than our own
so chosen home

TRUTH OR CONSEQUENCES

The statement
is followed

by the question
which is followed

by the searching
which allows

for research
which slows

to hypothesis
then theory

an example
a word problem

an equation
an answer

a reduction
an axiom

an equivalent
a symbol

a fact
I love you

a circuit
encircling us

we regret
our tendency

to tender
our memories

instead of the present
when I asked you

to sever your lessons
from your consequences

I meant
replace *sonorous*

with *generous*
precarious

fell that tree or make
a little room for me

among your nerve
endings and perseverations

and so present to me
a Pleiades of seeing

a limping sea
lion of a text

made of flesh
which should be

ceremoniously
undressed

if we are
to be blessed

and kissed
beset

by our very own
inconsequential sense

BEWILDERMENT

bewilder meant
to go beyond

to be past or
to unbetween

where no
poles rung

a song
like a bang

sung all
at once

in childhood
to be wilder

meant
the world

was piling up
if any how

a soaring in
disequilibrium

a fulcrum from
which come the stars

you saw from
swinging hard

bewilderment
is practice if

we can be full
of grace enough

that those who broke
the night into

unnumbered shards
could never fall

that we could grasp
a blade of grass

and see it fast
enough to know

and not forget
its increment

is ours
and set

ourselves to bending
large to small

this fulcrum
is a forge

in which we make
a wilder instrument

our stake
in this

remembrance
being infinite

a totalizing thrall
our evidence

for genuine
deliverance

from loneliness
to bewilder

is to join the wind
to hurricane right in

CEREMONY

When I was four I was a fire brigade,
a tree trunk, a lamp. When I was five

I was a station wagon, a pogo-stick,
an ice-cream truck. When I was six

ants covered my legs and I wore them
like trousers. When I was seven it began

to rain. When I was eight it stopped.
When I was nine I became a witness.

My hair was long. A ribbon snake
unhinged its jaw to swallow a fat toad.

When I was ten we blindfolded each other,
and you were there, but we couldn't see a thing.

When I was eleven we moved again. When I
was twelve you found me folded in a blanket on my roof.

No one else knew I was there. When I was thirteen
the house next door burned down. In the wreckage,

I found a photograph of you, a yearbook,
a broken cup. You fled the state. I followed

at fifteen (fourteen was a bad year) and found you
in a crumbling seaside hotel. You didn't see me,

lost in thought, considering time signatures
on the beach. When I was sixteen I spent

all the money I had. When I was seventeen
I passed you in the street and I looked like everyone.

You followed me, then grew distracted.
When I was eighteen I walked by the river

replicating the shapes of bushes. When I was nineteen
I left again. When I was twenty I was a groundskeeper,

a storehouse, a few states away. When I was twenty-one
I sold you a book and as you left the store I saw that look

on your face. When I was twenty-two you sat
a few rows behind me on someone's roof.

A movie flared on a screen. When I was twenty-
three we met on the subway, but I was sleeping

and you only stayed a few stops. When I was
twenty-four you left. So did I, but I saw you

around the neighborhood. When I was twenty-five
we frequented the parks. When I was twenty-six

I took a long nap and when I woke you told me
I'd been dreaming. When I was twenty-seven

you took this and folded it into a book.
When I was twenty-eight we demanded everything.

When I was twenty-nine we gladly accepted.
When I was thirty our delight came out

and we could not put it back. When I was
thirty-one our hunger went away and then returned.

When I was thirty-two my bad knee wept.
When I was thirty-three your flashlight failed.

When I was thirty-four you opened
tin cans with a fork. Lightning struck.

When I was thirty-five you told me
it wouldn't be too long, just wait.

When I was thirty-six our zealotry returned
and with it, fever. When I was thirty-seven our instincts

were right. When I was thirty-eight we gained another set.
When I was thirty-nine my plans for April were ruined,

but May was a success. When I was forty this
residual laughter, rain, a residue. When I was fifty this

resplendent cage of ribs, heart knocking itself
against its walls, still going. When I was sixty

your multiple decisions, industries, replies.
When I was seventy my overstated yes.

When I was eighty yes.
We agreed and disagreed. Yes.

II.

TO INHABIT

To curl up belongs to the phenomenology of the verb to inhabit
and only those who have learned to do so can inhabit with intensity.

GASTON BACHELARD

The Poetics of Space

1.

this seductive calm
belies a fire
roiling there
in the darker
quiet we have
no calm no
symmetry
a legion
of fecund
reasons and
two shoulders
squaring to
protect this
gentle paradox
we've yet
to name

2.

a latitude
where lions grow
more curious
descend their sand
colored hillsides
rivulets foaming
with sympathy
the lion comes
first then the
hillside follows

3.

perched like
crows in the
sky's highest
limbs so land
rolls its white
woolen rug
of winter
abominable
slowness
a flood
of yes

4.

after

the laughter

gets softer

you offer

a faster

return

5.

white horse laughing
in the snow
all its pieces
engender
a white cloud
exploding
in silence
in noise
a high sound
for a night
when we sigh
into sleep

6.

a sloop
asleep
in its slip
abreast
of a pulse
unspooled

7.

we crane
and go feathers
we fold
our forevers
together
to soften
their edges

8.

slow lightning
and thunder
bells woods
black bark
yellow leaf
and the tenderest
mushrooms
that follow
the rain

9.

the pines
lay down
their needles
in a gesture
that means
this bed
invites us
and so we
hold the trees
whose wrists
have whitened
with wind

10.

the cloud
that explodes
its quiet
furls open
like the looks
we can't count
and don't have to

11.

one fit

for winter

with yellow hair

that burns

the night

like hay

that tongues

the blanketed snow

and so beneath

each stalk

grown wild

in winter's

bone-white grip

lies a parcel

of crystalline feathers

grown long

and uncut

by the sun

12.

having come
to love
the questions
themselves

13.

with fever
we reach
hold on
with our
hands
and curve
into ever
again

14.

we outside in

the soft

sharp spot

the grace

of falling down

an avalanche

of now and then

the only thing

that's absolute

is yes

and yes

and yes

15.

in the falling
down dance
of the smoke
machine's chug
is a hush
made of magic
      a song
made of blood

16.

to narrow
to zero

    the throat
    full of muscle

a gift
in the air

    this will
    take you

a lifetime
of watching

    the object
    mid-arc

17.

your hand
releases

   its
   everything

and now
and again

   the arc
   flies right

this is
my beloved

   this is
   my

18.

we take
this pulse

effulgent

and flash
like a trick

star scudding

into bright
algal bloom

foaming green

in the ink-
dark sea

19.

into this
most dangerous

ocean we

enamor our
cuttlefish

we ink

our squid
and all

our mollusks fall
resplendently

as day

submits its fire
to night

20.

this is how
we do without
a common language

      mouth full
      of dark
      untellable color
      we forge
      a warmth
      from its black
      resilient flame

III.

YOU CAN
HAVE IT ALL

(VARIATIONS)

GENERATION

I am in the big green park which is green again and it is spring and I love
you and the park and the red birds in it. When you have birds in you

they are red and when it rains they eat enough for several years. Worms
become an offering to the sidewalks, or perhaps it is a performance,

two boys playing basketball, but it is really you and me who are
playing basketball but you are taller so you always win unless you let me

have the last word or one of yours. I would prefer that. Red birds are
positioning themselves in the field. They are coming closer and by the time

they get here, I am in my room looking through all my things wondering
where you are. How many charges we're going to get. I think you made the wind

blow harder because I hear something. If we get far enough south
we could grow new tongues, we could regard each other newly. When I mail this

it will contain paper and ink and those will make up a rendering of my house
just as they also make up certain declarations. I am not keeping anything

secret. Your night is becoming my morning and if we keep this up
we could be all the time in sunlight and even the weather wouldn't bother us.

RENDERING

I am in the big green park which is green again and it is spring and I love
where you are. How many charges do we get? You made the wind

have the last word or one of yours. I would prefer that red birds are
playing basketball but you are taller. So you always win unless you let me

become an offering to the sidewalks, or perhaps a performance,
a containment of paper and ink. Make-up, a rendering of my house,

which is red. When it rains they eat enough for several years. Worms have
you and the park and the red birds in it. When birds are in you they are

two boys playing basketball but it is really you and me who are
positioning themselves in the field. We are coming closer and by the time

we grow new tongues, we regard each other newly. When I mail this
secret, your night is becoming my morning and we keep

blowing harder because I hear something. If we get far enough south,
we could be all the time in sunlight and even the weather wouldn't bother us.

But it arrives, and I'm in my room looking through all my things. I wonder
if it makes certain declarations, weather. I am not keeping anything.

WARMING

We could be all the time in sunlight and even the weather wouldn't bother us.
You and the park and the red birds in it. When you have birds in you they are

an offering to the sidewalks, or perhaps a performance,
positions in the field. They are coming closer and by the time

I am in the big green park which is green again, it is spring and I love
playing basketball but you are taller so you always win unless you let me.

Blow harder because I hear something. If we get far enough south,
red and when it rains they eat enough for several years. Worms address

two boys playing basketball but it is really you and me who are
there, and we are getting charged. How many times have you made the wind

arrive? I'm in my room looking through all my things, wondering
how to make certain declarations like I am not keeping anything,

we could grow new tongues, we could regard each other newly. When I mail this,
please have the last word or one of yours. I would prefer that. Red birds are

secret. Your night is becoming my morning and if we keep this up
we will contain paper and ink. Those will make up a rendering of my house.

ANIMATION

Have the last word: it's one of yours. I would prefer that red birds are
in the big green park which is green again and it is spring and I love

containing paper and ink: those make up a rendering of my house
if we can be all the time in sunlight. Even the weather wouldn't bother

two boys playing basketball but it is really you and me who are
new tongues: we can regard each other newly when I mail this.

Blow harder because I hear something. If we get far enough south,
(secret: your night is becoming my morning) and if we keep this up,

(red) and when it rains. They eat enough for several years, worms,
just as they also make up certain declarations. I am not keeping anything

in the field. They are coming closer and by the time positions
arrive, I'm in my room looking through all my things wondering,

offering. The sidewalks are performing.
Where are you? And how. You are wind-charged,

the park, the red birds in it. When you have birds in you they
play basketball. You are taller so you always win. Unless you let me.

IV.

NUMEROUSNESS

Obsessed, bewildered

By the shipwreck
Of the singular

We have chosen the meaning
Of being numerous.

GEORGE OPPEN
"On Being Numerous"

MUTATIONS

I told L. it's strange
to know someone so well.

Someone else said art is
what you don't know you know

like how X becomes Y and now
there are eight hundred and fifty-seven

magnetic bones in my body
so itchy with kinetic sparks

I pace indoors, regard the radishes
chop them in two and cover

their vermillion hides with salt
but this is not anxiety.

Each day we invent new ways
of destroying ourselves and this too

is exhaling: particles moving off
in their tiny boats, violet and charged

toward each pole, which is how
we will get everything covered:

the earth is two-thirds water and
we have enough pieces to keep

sending them away forever.
All your previous lovers

will always want you.
All of mine still do.

Consider them satellites
and us the largest body on earth

which is known
for its reflective powers

and even more for the multitude
of species it sustains

never to be properly catalogued
never to be entirely known

which live in duplicitous broth
and multiply in utter dark

and also in a filtered light
that allows the accident wherein

something entirely different is born
climbing out of the sea:

the first turtle to battle an albatross
the first penguin to fly to its brothers

who stand, stunned
and bewildered on their rock.

THE MOST VIBRANT FORMS ARE EMERGENT FORMS

When we stood by ourselves we were okay.
We could make things for ourselves but

we wanted to make things for someone else.
We wanted others. But others meant

our okay was disrupted: we had to listen,
play well, laugh when others laughed.

We began to understand ourselves
in relation only to others and became

smaller, better, worse, smarter,
prettier, useless, crass, embarrassed,

fortunate, dumb. The people passed us
in their millions of shoes. Busses shouldered by

their payloads of strangers.
We were indifferent passengers.

We forgot how green
dresses the streets in May.

The insects remained asleep
in their private trees, who spoke

to their pale new buds
the way we folded

our arms over our chests.
Still. We had this feeling

our day would come.
We had to wait.

We had to do something.
Our fingers grew restless

and skittered over tabletops like mice.
We drew diagrams, plans, architectures.

We schemed and pitched
like underground dwellers

in the kind of colony
where everyone has a place.

We could feel the tunnel getting wider.
It opened like a hand holding a mouse in its palm.

We began to understand ourselves
in relation to our own diagrams,

the architectures we built for everyone.
We knew that one day

we would walk outside
and the sun would be there,

acting like it had never left.
We would be ready.

LOSSLESS

The end of a year
blurs into the next

as sound blurs to image
in the movies

we all get somewhere
we didn't know before

we walk into the dark
of the theater and take

our places before its
thrall and thank some

understood thing for
space shuttle car chase

and stranger arriving
to tell us what we've

always thought
was true the way

we ring in
New Year's Night

like its difference
was meant to signal

don't forget
these other years

we have been
before we walk

into another
darkened room

and there
is another

sleeping other
years and forming

the substance
for more

and more
never less

never less than we
already have.

THE LONGEST WINTER

There were days when we hoarded
our horticulture and ate our architecture.

We slept in a pasture of cygnets
when the clouds precipitated

into the horizon, a wheatfield
of news winging its way toward us

like a seagull, all business.
We were scared of scavengers.

Their industry implicated us.
If any *was* determined our *forth*,

it sorted itself in a private room
folding its letters and sending them

off in their tiny boats on their
private seas that flew the colors

of twilight in summer, lavenders,
sprays of pinks and slender greens.

India inks, seraphims.
We got all gothic

for a while, and shucked
those sleeves the way we shook

the sleep from our faces in the dark
mornings of the longest winters

which were all of them. If and when
we knew not what, we let things be

as they were, filled our canteens
and drank from them extravagantly

the last ones on earth, the very
favorite few, to whom it was left

to precipitate in the softest way
possible. We promised to snow.

THE VARIANT PITCH

today you leapt
for anything

I could throw
the wind

was a tonic
of nearby ocean

and you rained
laughter

if silence
had a form

mine would be
the white

buoyant bone
of the cuttlefish

and would whisper
over your body

recalcitrant sun
dealing out

unfathomable warmth
you slept beside me

your days unnumbered
not long enough

there is a song
asleep inside me

every ocean
has its understanding

oasis
in darkness

fragments of shells
how else

was I to tell you
but to shout?

TO SOUND LIKE SINGING

I'd like to describe
clouds instead

of people
their increase

up and out
blossoming

like the drawings
of William Kentridge

unfurling their subjects
ghosts posing

for portraits
as if they were

company
to cowboys

and the sunsets
they ride toward

to make sense
of the hurt

people put on
one another.

What is hate
but recognition?

When the opera
house arrived

a wealth
of baser music

came with it:
virtuosic noise

tomatoes / roses.
Singers afraid

of their audience.
On the front page

of the *New York Post*
a model holds a gun

to a man's jaw.
She's smiling.

They're in Moscow
on a runway.

We thrive
on contradiction.

In Florida,
in New York,

in California,
unarmed boys

are shot.
Men are jailed.

Clouds never *intend*.
Clouds are instruments

of great destruction.
Take the pine bark beetle,

who reddens
the evergreens,

who lays her eggs
beneath the bark

of ancient pines,
and makes of them

kindling for fires.
Once, they sailed

over the mountains
in the form of a cloud.

It was probably
beautiful.

THE LEFTOVERS

To be left over is to be transformed.
When next approached, the subjectivity

will have shifted, the tastebuds
and ocular mechanisms less prone

to the pleasures of the not-yet-left-
over the first time it was explored.

A shiver is the body receding
and not having enough room

to get away from itself. As if
we had invisibility cloaks

we could activate at will.
Switch off our presence

in any situation. When its wire
is tripped, the foghorn blares.

The foghorn is anchored
to its beam with metal bolts.

It will never go inside a house,
even though its steam puffs up

in such domestic shapes.
It offers heads of presidents,

horses, machine guns, Buicks.
The foghorn knows the world

we live in is alarming,
but it feels no kinship

with the siren. The foghorn's
vitality depends on the integrity

of the vessel on which it
perches like a parrot, aware

that the subjectivity it guards
may indeed be dangerous,

but it is a sublime danger.
The low, desolate, melancholic

noise the foghorn makes
is the sound of a subjectivity

calling out in the quiet
whiteness, *Look out,*

I'm about to arrive
on your shores.

THE BARRICADES

A jungle of flesh, flashing,
is a tolerable portion.

Embraced by a temporary edifice,
a parcel of bent dresses, braying.

In the streets they stop and slow,
photographing back to Ohio:

the mess parked like an idling car,
amassed, a scene couched in metal brackets.

A parenthetical, apparent
ethics (aside, an).

In the streets they come and go
dreaming of Joe DiMaggio, Brillo, the shows.

A piece of sidewalk set apart
for those who have stopped walking.

A contained derangement, hysterical
panoply. A fortified nerve bundle.

In the streets they catch and throw,
black boots and nightsticks swinging low.

A wrong order.
A flawed law.

Under certain circumstances,
the circuit dances.

The uncertain stance:
certainly sir we are permitted yes.

Now what
does a wrong law

lean on? The certain
dance: applause.

THE FEAST

We were the first ones here. We made sacrifices,
and we made ourselves comfortable. Our boredom

was not a topic of conversation. We redeemed each other
and so did not need to be saved and so we were saved.

We cashed in our friendships for two-person love.
We were told there would be others. We went

to find them, found no one. In the interim, we learned
to forage. We found supplies, which ran thin, so we formed

factions. For protection, for love, for comfort
against the other factions. Our scales went from one to ten.

We were of average height with extraordinary variations.
Our families were rich and fecund absences.

In the summertime, cloudscapes never failed
to entertain us. Daily our uncertainties rose up,

and we withdrew. We went behind the barn alone.
Climbed trees, drank. Built our forts and invited others

inside and made them leave when it suited us.
We invented systems of belonging that felt

valuable enough that we would want them.
We discarded each one as it revealed its flaws.

We wanted a new system. We wanted
a victory we would never be ashamed of.

We spoke in basements and kitchens.
We received gifts and we gave them away.

Suddenly, our hands were filled.
We laughed with our mouths open.

CONTINGENCIES

If any *is* is then
what is a thresh-

hold, what's
following us

into the next day?
A spot of shade

a cold river
a breeze

through a
railroad flat.

Doors will always
present themselves

coats opening
in darkness

fabric audibly
offering its

perceptual textures.
What is beauty worth?

A kind of tender
a currency

in perpetual flux
which is not to say

pattern recognition
is ignoble

compulsion a thing
we can hold

entirely away.
Reflection

is irrevocably
imaginative

which is not to say we
may ever hold ourselves

entirely apart.
Say love is an agreement.

Say it's more
about the confluence

of our beginnings
that can never be

otherwise created
an effect of always

otherwise.
Do you choose

how you love?
Abandon

all otherwise rivers
breezes through other flats

the railroads forgotten
erased?

The you you were
is the starting gun

the clay, the doll
inside the larger doll.

Love is a condition.
There are no agreements

only the fraught joy
of taking out the smaller doll

firing the starting gun
and starting, again, to run.

ACKNOWLEDGMENTS

My enduring gratitude goes to the editors of the journals and presses who published many of these poems: *Spork, Diner, Seattle Review, Big Bell, New Orleans Review, Konundrum Literary Engine Review, Epiphany, Lyre Lyre, Jubilat,* and All Along Press. The section, "To Inhabit," was published as a chapbook by Ugly Duckling Presse in October 2012, under the title, *20 Love Poems for 10 Months.*

The title, "The Most Vibrant Forms are Emergent Forms" was taken from Dean Young's poem, "Whale Watch." "The Feast" was written for F.E.A.S.T., an arts-funding dinner held in Greenpoint, Brooklyn. The section "To Inhabit," "Origin Story," and "Truth or Consequences" were written for Chris Martin. "The Longest Winter," "Mutations," and "You Can Have It All" were written for Russell Dillon.

I am indebted to the following people whose generosity helped to bring these poems to fruition in one way or another: the brilliant Chris Martin, Kramer O'Neill, Misty Harper, Sara Jane Stoner, Russell Dillon, Michael Loughran, Kaveh Bassiri, Greg Hewett, Mary Hickman, Callie Garnett, Margaret Ross, Dan Poppick, Katherine Bogden Bayard and Joseph Massey.

My additional thanks go to Matthea Harvey for her warm and thoughtful introduction and her fantastic poetry, Peter Gizzi and Anna Moschovakis for their brave and important work and their kind words about mine, and to the magical people at Slope Editions—Christopher Janke, Ethan Paquin, Evan White, Kate Litterer and the inimitable Kelin Loe—for the opportunity to design my own book and the attention, enthusiasm and support to get it out into the world.

And to my family, whose support and love of words and music made these poems possible, and my teachers, Marilyn Hacker, Kevin Young and Maurice Manning, for teaching me to read more generously. Thank you.

ABOUT THE AUTHOR

Mary Austin Speaker is the author of the chapbooks *The Bridge* (Push Press 2011), and *20 Love Poems for 10 Months* (Ugly Duckling Presse 2012); and a play, *I Am You This Morning You Are Me Tonight* (Bridge 2012) written with her husband, the poet Chris Martin. She co-founded the Triptych poetry reading series in New York City in 2008 and curated the Reading Between A&B series for several years. Her critical work has appeared recently in *Pleiades, Painted Bride Quarterly* and elsewhere. She lives in Iowa City, IA and operates a tiny design studio.